This book belongs to…

D1484058

Pronunciation Guide

Aajee – Aa–jee

Aajobaa – Aa–jo–baa

Aparna – Uh–purr–naa

Chaturthi – Chu–toor–ththee

Ganpati Bappa Morya – Gan–puh–tee Bup–pa Mow–ray–yaa

Ganesha – Guh–nay–shaa

Kartik – Caar–teek

Lal Baug cha Raja – Laal Baag chaa Raajaa

Lezim – Lay–jhim

Mandap – Mun–dup

Marathi – Muh–raa–ththi

Parvati – Par–vuh–tee

Tasha – Taa–shaa

Visarjan – Vee–sir–juhn

Note for parents: Our books provide a glimpse into the beautiful cultural diversity of India, including occasional mythology references. Given India's size and diversity, Ganesh Chaturthi (birthday) is celebrated in a multitude of different ways. In this book, we showcase elements of Ganesh Chaturthi that are best suited for young readers to follow.

Let's Celebrate Ganesha's Birthday!

Raise Multicultural Kids

Written by:
Ajanta & Vivek

This is a map of India. India is a big country. It has many states, languages, festivals, and dances.

Do you see the red star on the map? That is Mumbai.

People in Mumbai celebrate Ganesha's birthday with a big festival. A lot of people in Mumbai speak a language called Marathi.

On a beautiful morning, Maya, Neel and Chintu arrive at their friend Aparna's house in Mumbai. Aparna lives with her grandparents.

In Marathi, Grandma is called Aajee and grandpa is called Aajobaa. Aparna is very excited to see her friends and gives them big hugs.

Aajee says "Kids, you are just in time for Ganesha's 10-day birthday celebration. The first day is called Ganesh Chaturthi."

"Who is Ganesha, Aajee?" the kids ask. Aajee smiles. She opens her big book of Ganesha stories and reads to them.

Who is Ganesha?

Some people in India pray to Ganesha as a God. Ganesha has the head of an elephant and a fun pot belly. Look carefully at his tusks. Can you tell one is shorter than the other?

People believe Ganesha is the son of God Shiva and Goddess Parvati. He also has a brother named Kartik.

Ganesha loves to eat a yummy dessert called Modak. It has a fun shape.

Ganesha rides a mouse. People believe Ganesha takes their troubles away.

Ganesha's mouse helps him travel to every little corner of the world to help people.

Ganesha's Elephant Head

One day, Parvati was getting ready for her bath. She needed someone to guard the place. She made a beautiful boy out of clay and magically put life into him. This little boy was Ganesha.

Shiva came to meet Parvati. Shiva and Ganesha did not know each other. Ganesha stopped the mighty Shiva from going inside. Shiva got very angry.

They got into a fight and Shiva accidentally hurt Ganesha in the head. Shiva felt very bad for Ganesha and promised to get him a new head.

Shiva was determined to find Ganesha a new head. After looking for a long time, Shiva found a beautiful head of an elephant. He placed it on Ganesha's neck.

Because Ganesha was so brave, Shiva also asked everyone to pray to Ganesha for good luck.

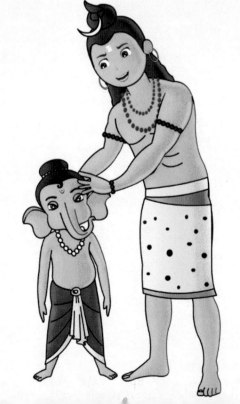

"Today is Ganesh Chaturthi," Aparna exclaims the next morning "Let's get a Ganesha statue to celebrate his birthday".

Aparna and Aajee take the kids on a double decker bus ride.

All of Mumbai is preparing for the festival.

They see a massive structure with colorful decorations.

"This is called a mandap," Aparna explains "This is where they will put a big Ganesha statue."

How big is the statue if it needs such a big house? Neel wonders.

The bus arrives at a big workshop. It is a magical place. They see rows and rows of Ganesha statues in many poses.

Some are dancing. Some are sitting down. Some are tiny. Some are very tall.

Workers are busy with the statues. Some are mixing clay. Some are making the shape of the statues. Some are painting the statues.

Aparna buys a smaller statue for their home. They are all very excited. Chintu claps his hands with joy and they head back home.

Aajobaa meets them back home. He decorates a table with pretty flowers, lamps and colorful lights.

He, then, carefully places the Ganesha statue in the middle.

"Did you know Ganesha is considered to be very smart?" He asks.

"Let me tell you how Ganesha won a race simply by being smart", Aajee says. The kids can't wait to hear the story.

Ganesha wins the race

Once, Ganesha and his brother, Kartik were fighting over a precious fruit. They both wanted to eat it.

To help decide who would get to eat it they went to their parents, Shiva and Parvati. Their parents gave them a challenge. They told them to race around the world three times. The winner of the race would win the fruit.

Kartik immediately climbed his ride, a peacock.
He flew away at a fast pace.

Ganesha was in trouble. His ride, a mouse,
couldn't keep up with Kartik's fast-flying
peacock.

Instead, he came up with
a clever idea. He started
to run around his
parents.

Shiva and Parvati were confused. They asked Ganesha why he was
running around them. Ganesha replied with a smile, "My parents are
like my whole world. So if I run around you, it is as if I ran around the
whole world".

Shiva and Parvati were very impressed. They declared Ganesha the
winner.

The next morning the kids dress up in fancy clothes. They come across a street with dancers and drummers.

"This dance is called Lezim. The drum is called Dhol Tasha," Aparna explains.

The drums are loud and powerful. The dancers are energetic; twisting, turning and bouncing. The kids even try out a few dance moves. They love it!

"Are you ready for a really cool adventure?" Aparna asks. Her eyes shine with excitement. "YES!" Maya, Neel and Chintu scream.

Aparna takes them to a massive hall. It is packed with people. Maya, Neel and Chintu's jaws drop.

"Whoa, whoa, whoa!" Neel shakes his head to see if he is dreaming. In front of them is a Ganesha statue that is **2** houses tall!

"This place is called Lal Baug cha Raja," Aparna explains. Sound of drums, bells and chants fill the air.

Maya and Neel look around in wonder. "Yes, the coolest adventure so far" Maya whispers.

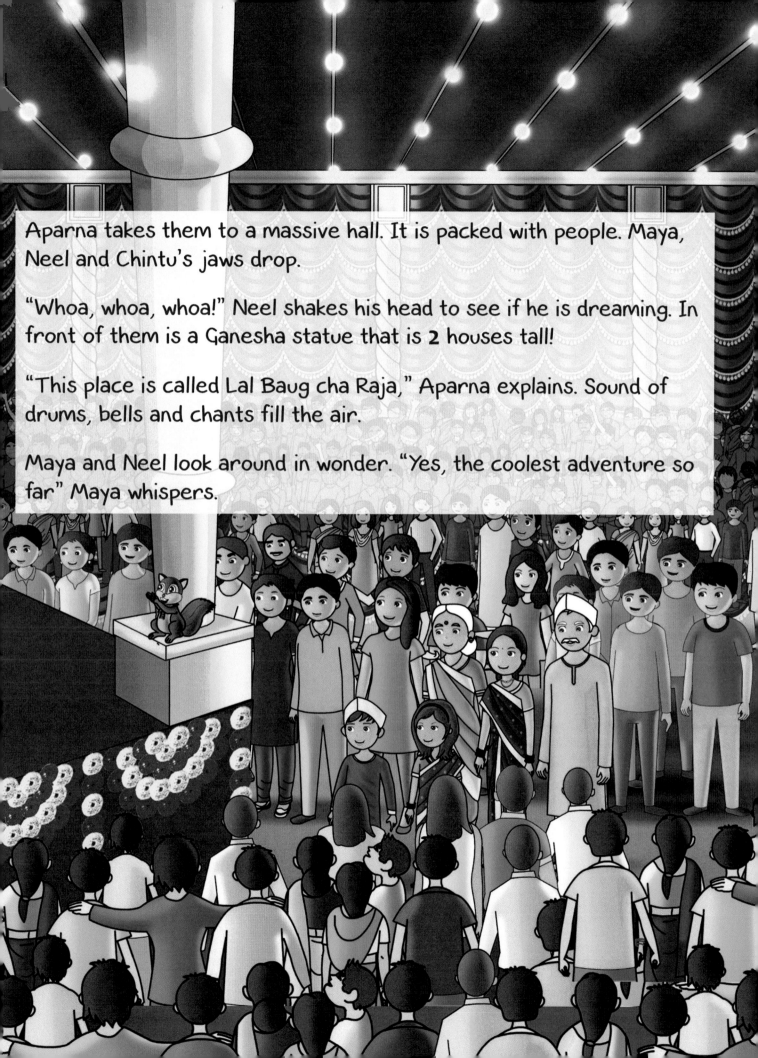

A few days later, they see Aajobaa and Aajee wrapping up the statue.

"What is happening?" Maya asks.

"Ten days of celebration is over. It's time to put the statue in water. This is called Visarjan," Aajobaa explains.

"Ganpati Bappa Morya!" Aparna cheers. "This is what you say as you take the statue for Visarjan," Aparna explains, "It means may Ganesha bless us".

"Ganpati Bappa Morya!" Everyone cheers together and they head out.

Maya and Neel cannot believe their eyes.

The street is packed with people carrying statues. Some are small. Some are very, very big.

People are clapping, dancing and singing "Ganpati Bappa Morya!" Chintu hops on the statue and sings as well.

After a long walk, they arrive at a beach. They see people putting statues in the water.

They walk among them and put their statue in as well. It is a bittersweet moment.

"The clay of the statue mixes with water," Aparna says.

"People believe when this happens, Ganesha goes back to his parents' house in the mountains."

"Wow! That was one amazing adventure," Maya says.

"Yes, we had so much fun celebrating Ganesha's birthday!" Neel says.

Chintu nods. He does a happy squirrel dance.

"We cannot wait for our next adventure. I wonder where that will be. We hope you can join us then!" Maya, Neel, and Chintu say.

"Until then, Namaste!"

Let's look back on our wonderful trip to celebrate Ganesha's B'Day

Whose birthday are we celebrating? *Ganesha's*

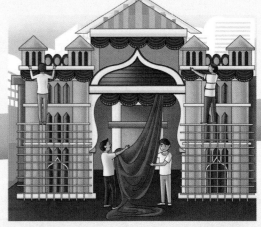

What is the festival called? *Ganesh Chaturthi*

What is the fun dance called? *Lezim*

What is the name of the place with the gigantic Ganesha statue? *Lal Baug cha raja*

For how many days is Ganesh Chaturthi celebrated? *Ten*

Who are Ganesha's Mom & Dad? *Parvati and Shiva*

What is Ganesha's favorite dessert? *Modak*

What animal is Ganesha's ride? *Mouse*

What do they cheer when they taking the statue to water? *Ganpati Bappa Morya*

What is putting the statues in water called? *Visarjan*

About the Authors

Ajanta Chakraborty was born in Bhopal, India, and moved to North America in 2001. She earned an MS in Computer Science from the University of British Columbia and also earned a Senior Diploma in Bharatanatyam, a classical Indian dance, to feed her spirit.

Ajanta quit her corporate consulting job in 2011 and took the plunge to run Bollywood Groove (and also Culture Groove) full-time. The best part of her work day includes grooving with classes of children as they leap and swing and twirl to a Bollywood beat.

Vivek Kumar was born in Mumbai, India, and moved to the US in 1998. Vivek has an MS in Electrical Engineering from The University of Texas, Austin, and an MBA from the Kellogg School of Management, Northwestern University.

Vivek has a very serious day job in management consulting. But he'd love to spend his days leaping and swinging, too.

We have been featured on:

We are independent authors who want to help raise multicultural kids and create a more tolerant world! We will greatly appreciate your support:

1.   Drop us an Amazon review at: **CultureGroove.com/books**

2.   **Subscribe** to our multicultural video channel featuring Maya, Neel & Chintu: **CultureGroove.com/youtube**

3.   Tell your friends

Many thanks!

Made in the USA
Lexington, KY
21 June 2019